RAILWAYS IN SOUTH WALES AND THE CENTRAL WALES LINE

IN THE LATE 20TH CENTURY

RAILWAYS IN SOUTH WALES AND THE CENTRAL WALES LINE

IN THE LATE 20TH CENTURY

PETER J. GREEN

PEN & SWORD
TRANSPORT

AN IMPRINT OF PEN & SWORD BOOKS LTD.
YORKSHIRE – PHILADELPHIA

First published in Great Britain in 2022 by
Pen and Sword Transport
An imprint of
Pen & Sword Books Ltd.
Yorkshire - Philadelphia

ISBN 978 1 39908 654 7

Typeset by SJmagic DESIGN SERVICES, India.

Printed and bound by Printworks Global Ltd, London / Hong Kong.

Pen & Sword Books Ltd incorporates the Imprints of Pen & Sword Books Archaeology, Atlas,
Aviation, Battleground, Discovery, Family History, History, Maritime, Military, Naval, Politics,
Railways, Select, Transport, True Crime, Fiction, Frontline Books, Leo Cooper, Praetorian Press,
Seaforth Publishing, Wharncliffe and White Owl.

For a complete list of Pen & Sword titles please contact

PEN & SWORD BOOKS LIMITED
47 Church Street, Barnsley, South Yorkshire, S70 2AS, England
E-mail: enquiries@pen-and-sword.co.uk
Website: www.pen-and-sword.co.uk

or

PEN AND SWORD BOOKS
1950 Lawrence Rd, Havertown, PA 19083, USA
E-mail: Uspen-and-sword@casematepublishers.com
Website: www.penandswordbooks.com

CONTENTS

INTRODUCTION

Following the end of steam on British Railways in the 1960s, my railway interest turned to overseas steam, steam specials, and preserved railways, particularly the narrow gauge railways of Wales. I also made regular visits to Barry where I would wander among the rows of derelict steam locomotives at Woodham Brothers' scrapyard, cheered only by the increasing number that had been targeted for preservation. From time to time during my weekend visits, I would see diverted iron ore trains, hauled by triple-headed Class 37 diesels, pass through Barry station, but in those days I was not motivated to point my cameras in their direction. I did, however, make a few trips to Devon to see the Western Class diesels, bringing back memories of my earlier trainspotting days.

With a change in personal circumstances in 1981, I began to take more of an interest in the modern railway scene, concentrating on the activity around my home town of Worcester, as well as those centres of railway activity that were easily reached by rail or road. Steam specials were not neglected and frequent visits were made to the Settle and Carlisle Line and the Welsh Marches. Early starts were usual, in order to take in some diesel operations before the steam locomotive appeared.

After a time, I started to make more trips purely to photograph diesel action. In those days there was far more railway infrastructure and mechanical signalling, as well as a greater variety of traffic and motive power than there is today and the general railway scene was, at least for me, far more interesting.

Newport and Cardiff quickly became favourite destinations, providing reasonable levels of freight traffic at weekends, to which most of my visits were limited because of work commitments. They were also within easy reach of Worcester, the journey by road taking less than an hour and a half.

I soon started taking an interest in the colliery traffic which often involved taking days or, on a few occasions, weeks off work. I found these operations particularly interesting, not least because the normal motive power was the Class 37 diesel, which has long been a personal favourite of mine.

As time went on, collieries closed and the coal traffic reduced, but there always seemed to be something new to interest me. Rugby Internationals at Cardiff always produced a number of special trains which arrived from various parts of the country, often bringing interesting motive power to the Welsh capital.

The Rhymney Valley also saw Class 37 diesels working passenger trains into the twenty-first century and, on Rugby International days, privately-owned Class 50s were also used on occasions. Of course, all this attracted many enthusiasts who came to ride on and photograph the trains.

The Class 37s were replaced by Class 56s, and later Class 60s on many duties in South Wales, but today it is still possible to experience a Class 37 growling up a Welsh valley on the Pontypool and Blaenavon Railway.

I also enjoyed the Central Wales line very much, particularly the visits I made before the semaphore signals were replaced. In those days I found the small country stations pleasant places to spend a few hours.

In making my selection of photos for this book, most of which were taken in the 1980s and 1990s until around the turn of the century, I have tried to provide good coverage of the railways and trains in the southern part of Wales during this time period. To bring the story a little more up to date, I have also included a short section showing something of the preserved railways in the area in recent years.

Peter J. Green
Worcester, England
2022

ACKNOWLEDGEMENTS

I n the 1980s and 1990s, much of my spare time was spent photographing railways and, in the 1990s in particular, a lot of my holidays were used up on overseas trips to the railway systems of various countries. One consequence of this was that I did not visit South Wales during the normal working week quite as often as I would have liked.

Fortunately, both Paul Dorney and Steve Turner have come to my rescue and have allowed me to use their pictures of those parts of the railway that I did not manage to photograph myself. It was Paul who originally encouraged me to take an interest in the railways associated with the collieries of South Wales, for which I am very grateful, and both he and Steve have also helped me with information for the captions of various photographs of my own.

I only made one brief and unsuccessful visit to photograph Margam Yard and the workings to and from Port Talbot Steelworks, but Rob Pritchard has helped me with two photographs taken during a visit in 1999.

James Billingham, who often accompanied me on my visits, has also given me considerable help with many of the captions.

In addition, Don Gatehouse, Martin Loader, David Rostance and Bob Sweet have each provided answers to some of my most difficult questions.

For information relating to the various industrial locomotives that appear in these pages, I am indebted to members of the Industrial Railway Society group at: IndustrialRailwaySociety@groups.io

Val Brown has, as usual, checked and corrected the many errors in my text.

My thanks go to you all.

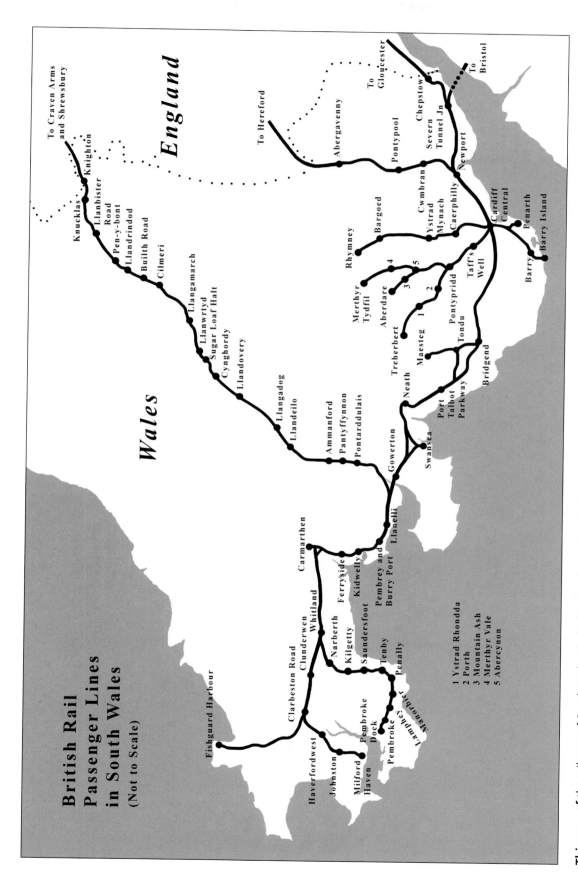

British Rail Passenger Lines in South Wales
(Not to Scale)

England

Wales

To Craven Arms and Shrewsbury

Knighton
Knucklas
Llanbister Road
Pen-y-bont
Llandrindod
Builth Road
Cilmeri
Llangamarch
Llanwrtyd
Sugar Loaf Halt
Cynghordy
Llandovery
Llangadog
Llandeilo
Ammanford
Pantyffynnon
Pontarddulais
Gowerton
Swansea

To Hereford

Abergavenny
To Gloucester
Pontypool
Severn Tunnel Jn
Chepstow
To Bristol
Newport

Rhymney
Bargoed
Cwmbran
Ystrad Mynach
Caerphilly
Cardiff Central
Penarth
Barry Island
Barry

Merthyr Tydfil
Aberdare
4
3 5
1 2
Treherbert
Maesteg
Neath
Pontypridd
Tondu
Taff's Well
Bridgend
Port Talbot Parkway

Carmarthen
Ferryside
Kidwelly
Pembrey and Burry Port
Llanelli

Fishguard Harbour
Clarbeston Road
Clunderwen
Whitland
Narberth
Kilgetty
Saundersfoot
Tenby
Penally
Manorbier

Haverfordwest
Johnston
Milford Haven
Pembroke Dock
Pembroke
Lamphey

1 Ystrad Rhondda
2 Porth
3 Mountain Ash
4 Merthyr Vale
5 Abercynon

This map of the railways of South Wales, including the Central Wales line, shows the British Rail passenger lines that were operational during the period covered by this book. Many stations have been omitted for clarity.

1. English Electric Type 3 diesel-electrics 37508 and 37511 slowly move their train under the loader at Deep Navigation Colliery, Treharris, as it is filled with coal for Aberthaw Power Station. The colliery, opened in 1872, was closed in 1991. 14 July 1986.

NEWPORT TO THE ENGLISH BORDER

2. From Newport in South Wales there are three railway routes to England. These run to Hereford to the north, to Gloucester via Chepstow, and to Bristol and London via the Severn Tunnel. Here, Class 66 66117 heads a westbound empty stone train through Newport station, a little over 133 miles from London Paddington by rail. 13 October 2001.

3. On the day of a rugby match at Cardiff, English Electric Type 3 37038 crosses the River Usk and approaches Newport station with the 08.33 Manchester Piccadilly to Cardiff Central. Newport Castle is to the right of the river bridge. 20 May 2000.

4. Brush Type 4 47613 *North Star* crosses the River Usk as it heads away from the Newport station stop towards Maindee West Junction with the 09.50 Swansea to Portsmouth Harbour. 5 March 1988.

5. Viewed from Pillmawr Road, the diesel multiple unit (DMU) forming a Cardiff Central to Hereford service crosses the River Usk for the second time since leaving Newport, as it heads away from Maindee North Junction towards Caerleon. 5 March 1988.

6. Carrying the West Highland Terrier emblem of Glasgow Eastfield Traction Maintenance Depot (TMD), 37407 *Loch Long* passes Ponthir with the 15.00 Cardiff Central to Rhyl. 29 April 1989.

7. **Passing British** Steel Corporation's Panteg Steelworks, 37428 *David Lloyd George* heads for Newport with the 1V02 06.20 Crewe to Cardiff Central. The works closed in 2004. 5 March 1988.

8. **Running alongside** the A4042 dual carriageway, 37429 *Eisteddfod Genedlaethol* approaches Pontypool station with the 1M17 13.23 Cardiff Central to Liverpool Lime Street. The station was named Pontypool Road until 1972 and became Pontypool and New Inn in 1994. 29 April 1989.

9. Birmingham Railway Carriage and Wagon Company (BRCW) Type 3 33064 approaches Pontypool station as it heads north with the 1M75 15.10 Cardiff Central to Crewe. 16 April 1983.

10. Class 37/9 diesel-electrics 37903 and 37904 head an empty southbound steel train through Pontypool station. These locomotives were rebuilds of 37249 and 37124 and were fitted with Mirrlees MB275T engines. 29 April 1989.

11. Class 37/9 37906 approaches Little Mill signal box with the 8Z18 Severn Tunnel Junction to Hereford permanent way train. The Great Western Railway (GWR) Little Mill Junction signal box was a McKenzie and Holland Type 3 design, built in 1883 at the junction of the lines to Newport, Hereford and Usk. The Class 37/9, rebuilt from 37206, is fitted with a Ruston RK270T engine. 28 February 1987.

12. Brush Type 4 47442 passes Little Mill with the 07.10 Manchester Piccadilly to Cardiff Central. The freight line to Glascoed Royal Ordnance Factory, previously the line to Usk and Coleford, is curving away to the right. 28 February 1987.

13. Metro-Cammell Class 101 DMU set C852, forming a Hereford to Cardiff Central service, passes the old station building at Penpergwm. The station closed in 1958. 12 March 1988.

14. Class 37/9 37903 heads a southbound loaded steel coil train through Abergavenny. 13 June 1987.

15. Brush Type 4 47360 heads a southbound tank train through Abergavenny. Opened in 1854, the station was named Abergavenny Monmouth Road between 1950 and 1968. A branch line to Brynmawr from Abergavenny Junction station, located further north, opened in 1862. 6 July 1985.

16. BRCW Type 3 33065 arrives at Abergavenny with the 1M84 11.40 Cardiff Central to Crewe. Abergavenny signal box, on the left, is a GWR Type 28b design, dating from 1934. 26 November 1983.

17. A two-car DMU, forming a Hereford to Cardiff Central service, runs down Llanvihangel Bank towards Abergavenny. Llanvihangel Bank climbs north from Abergavenny at a 1 in 82 gradient to the summit near Llanvihangel station. 12 March 1988.

18. Brush Type 4 47543 approaches the site of Llanvihangel station at Llanvihangel Crucorney with the 05.15 Holyhead to Cardiff Central. The station closed in 1958. 26 March 1988.

19. After passing Hereford and heading into Wales, English Electric Type 3 37904 heads a southbound loaded steel coil train past Pandy. 26 March 1988.

20. Heading east from Newport, 60093 *John Stirk* passes East Usk Yard with an iron ore train from Port Talbot to Llanwern Steelworks. The semaphore signal controls access to the freight line from East Usk Junction to Uskmouth. 4 April 1994.

21. British Rail Type 5 Co-Co diesel-electric 60092 *Reginald Munns*, built by Brush Traction, heads a loaded steel train away from Llanwern Steelworks and on to the main line to Newport. 30 December 1994.

22. BRCW Type 3 33062 passes Undy, between Llanwern and Severn Tunnel Junction, with Sunday's 1O87 16.05 Cardiff Central to Portsmouth Harbour via the Severn Tunnel. The locomotive will be replaced at Bristol Temple Meads. 12 June 1983.

23. The line to Chepstow and Gloucester and the line to Bristol and London via the Severn Tunnel divide at Severn Tunnel Junction. Here, a DMU, forming the 16.00 Chepstow to Cardiff Central service, departs from Severn Tunnel Junction station. 20 July 1985.

24. Diverted from its usual route via the Severn Tunnel, the InterCity 125 unit forming the 10.00 Swansea to London Paddington is about to pass under the 'old' Severn Bridge as it heads towards Chepstow and Gloucester. 26 February 1995.

25. The DMU forming the 14.39 Chepstow to Cardiff Central service waits for departure time from Chepstow. The station was completed in 1850 and the GWR cast-iron footbridge, with its wooden cladding and canopy, was cast at Edward Finch's ironworks, next to the station. It is a Grade II listed structure. 17 November 1990.

26. Metro-Cammell Class 101 DMU set C805 passes the old goods shed as it departs from Chepstow. Although the destination indicator says Gloucester, the train is heading for Newport and Cardiff. 28 June 1986.

27. With the construction of the A48 road bridge in progress on the right, a six-car DMU, forming the 17.05 Cardiff Central to Gloucester, crosses the River Wye as it heads away from Chepstow to England. Chepstow station can be seen in the background. The railway bridge superstructure replaced that of Brunel's bridge of 1852. The tubular iron supports still remain. 28 June 1986.

AROUND NEWPORT

28. On the occasion of a Rugby International at Cardiff's Millennium Stadium, split-box Class 37s 37029 and 37038 depart from Newport station with the 08.33 Manchester Piccadilly to Cardiff Central. The leading locomotive, 37029, now preserved, carries the 1V70 headcode and has the small version of the West Highland Terrier emblem of Glasgow Eastfield TMD on its bodyside. 13 October 2001.

29. After departing from Newport, 37425 *Sir Robert McAlpine/Concrete Bob* leads the 09.14 Liverpool Lime Street to Cardiff Central towards Gaer Junction. The train has just exited the newer of the Hillfield Tunnels, built in 1912. The other tunnel is Brunel's South Wales Railway tunnel of 1850. The two parallel tunnels are 2,226ft long. 20 February 1993.

30. Sulzer Type 4 'Peak' 1Co-Co1 diesel-electric 45130 heads a Portsmouth Harbour to Cardiff Central service out of the newer of the Hillfield Tunnels at Newport. The 'Peak' will have taken over the train at Bristol Temple Meads. 11 October 1986.

31. Class 59 3,300hp Co-Co diesel-electric locomotive 59002 *Alan J Day* passes Gaer Junction with iron ore empties from Llanwern Steelworks to Port Talbot. On the right, 37701 waits for the road with a freight from Hallam Marsh to Alexandra Dock Junction Yard. The first four Class 59 locomotives were built by Electro-Motive Diesel (EMD), USA, for Foster Yeoman Ltd, near Frome, Somerset and were delivered in January 1986. 12 July 1997.

32. Class 56 Co-Co diesel-electric 56128 leads a westbound empty steel train out of Alexandra Dock Junction Yard. Scrap steel wagons are behind the two hood wagons at the front of the train. On the left, Class 158 Sprinter 158 834 passes Ebbw Junction as it heads for Cardiff Central. 6 December 1997.

33. In April 1986, the Monmouthshire Railway Society ran 'The Risca Cuckoo' railtour from Newport to various destinations in the area, including Newport Dock Street and Rose Heyworth Colliery. Here, after visiting Dock Street, the railtour, with Class 116 DMU set C306 leading, pauses at Iron Gates level crossing on Commercial Road as it heads back to Alexandra Dock Junction and on to Machen Quarry. 5 April 1986.

34. With Newport's Transporter Bridge in the background, 37162 shunts a coal train at Dock Street Sidings. Opened in 1906, the bridge is one of only six operational transporter bridges left in the world out of the twenty constructed. 23 August 1988. (*Paul Dorney Photo*)

35. Class 59 diesel-electric 59001 *Yeoman Endeavour* heads an empty iron ore train, from Llanwern Steelworks to Port Talbot, past Alexandra Dock Junction Yard. Ebbw Junction is on the left. Built at La Grange, Illinois, USA, these locomotives were based on EMD's successful SD40-2 model, of which over 4,000 were built. 10 May 1997.

36. In early Network SouthEast livery, 50019 *Ramillies* passes Ebbw Junction at Newport with the 14.51 Bristol Temple Meads to Cardiff Central. The former Newport Ebbw Junction TMD, closed in 1983, is on the left. 23 May 1987.

THE NEWPORT VALLEYS

Above: **37. After leaving** the South Wales main line at Gaer Junction, English Electric Type 3 37230 approaches Park Junction with an empty ballast train, bound for Machen Quarry. At Park Junction, the lines from Gaer Junction and Ebbw Junction meet and the freight line to Machen diverges from the line to Ebbw Vale. The siding in the foreground is a remnant of the route which once led to the Town Dock. 11 October 1986.

Opposite above: **38. English Electric** Type 3 37248 passes Park Junction signal box with a loaded coal train from Marine Colliery to Radyr. Park Junction signal box is a Type 3 McKenzie & Holland design, built for the GWR in 1885. The box was later extended. 11 October 1986.

Opposite below: **39. English Electric** Type 3 37244 heads north at Rogerstone with an empty coal train from Llanwern to Marine Colliery. The old Rogerstone station building is behind the locomotive. The station was closed in 1968 and a new station, located about ½ mile north of the original station, opened in 2008. This line replaced a double track line on the alignment of the new road. 7 April 1987.

40. Running next to the A467 dual carriageway, Class 37/9 37901 *Mirrlees Pioneer* passes Rogerstone as it heads south with an empty steel train from Ebbw Vale. Rogerstone Power Station, in the background, closed in 1984. 7 April 1987.

41. Lime Kiln Junction, near Risca, is the junction of the lines to Newport, Ebbw Vale and Oakdale Colliery. The GWR signal box was closed in 2007. In May 1987, Pathfinder Tours ran 'The Gwent Valley Explorer' railtour from Crewe to Ebbw Vale, Machen, Barry Island and Oakdale Colliery using Class 40 D200. After visiting Oakdale Colliery, D200/40122 is pictured at Lime Kiln Junction on its way back to Newport and Crewe. 23 May 1987.

42. English Electric Type 3 37244 approaches the level crossing at Oakdale Colliery as it arrives with coal empties from Llanwern. 7 April 1987.

43. Oakdale Colliery, opened in 1911 in the Sirhowy Valley, was closed in 1989. Here, Class 37 37284 is pictured slowly running under the loader as its train is filled with coal for Llanwern Steelworks. 7 April 1987.

44. English Electric Type 4 40122, previously D200, stands in the late afternoon sunshine at Oakdale Colliery with Pathfinder Tours' 'The Gwent Valley Explorer' railtour from Crewe. 23 May 1987.

45. North of Lime Kiln Junction, near Newbridge on the line to Ebbw Vale, was Celynen South Colliery. The colliery closed in November 1985 but much still remained in April 1986. Here, viewed from the platform of Celynen South Halt, the DMU working the 'The Risca Cuckoo' railtour is heading south past the closed colliery. The two shunters standing in the colliery are North British (NB) 0-4-0 diesel-hydraulics 28040 (no. 2) and 28027 (no. 1). NB 28027, built in 1960, is former British Railways D2774. It has since been preserved at the Strathspey Railway. 5 April 1986.

46. To the north of Celynen South Colliery was Celynen North. Here, 37303 passes with a loaded coal train from Marine Colliery to Llanwern. For its last few years, the colliery was linked underground to Oakdale, where the coal was raised to the surface. The colliery closed in 1989. 14 May 1987.

47. A number of Class 122 single-unit railcars saw service as route learners. Here, TDB 975023 is on route learning duty at Aberbeeg. Previously British Railways' W55001, the railcar is now preserved at the East Lancashire Railway. Aberbeeg Junction signal box, in the background, was a GWR Type 5 box, built in 1891. It closed in 1997. 7 April 1987.

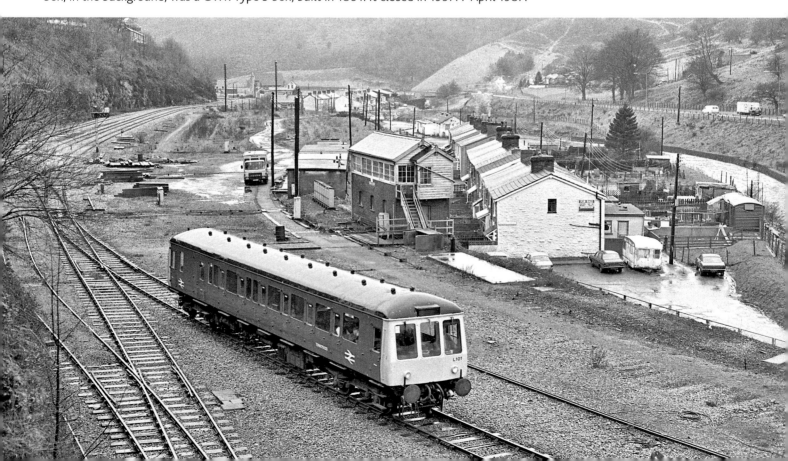

48. Aberbeeg was the junction of the lines to Newport, Ebbw Vale and Rose Heyworth. Here, 37901 *Mirrlees Pioneer* stands opposite Aberbeeg Junction signal box with a steel train to Ebbw Vale Steelworks. The Class 37 was built at Vulcan Foundry in 1963 as D6850, becoming 37150 in 1974. Rebuilt at Crewe, it re-entered service in late 1986 as 37901. 7 April 1987.

49. English Electric Type 3 37289 runs through the platforms of the abandoned station as it rounds the curve at Aberbeeg with a loaded coal train from Marine Colliery to Llanwern. The Ebbw River and the Ebbw Fach River meet at Aberbeeg as can be seen to the left of the old station. 7 April 1987.

50. The Monmouthshire Railway Society's 'The Risca Cuckoo' railtour from Newport visited the closed Rose Heyworth Colliery in April 1986. Here the railtour, with Class 116 DMU set C306 leading, stands at the colliery at the end of the branch line from Aberbeeg. Rose Heyworth Colliery, opened in 1872, was named after the wife of Lawrence Heyworth, the first managing director of the South Wales Colliery Company. The colliery closed in October 1985. 5 April 1986.

51. Marine Colliery was located at Cwm, north of Aberbeeg on the line to Ebbw Vale. Here, 37901 *Mirrlees Pioneer* passes the colliery with a steel train to Ebbw Vale. Marine, the last deep mine in the Ebbw valleys, closed in March 1989. 7 April 1987.

52. English Electric Type 3 37252 is pictured heading north, at the coal mining village of Cwm, with a steel train to Ebbw Vale. 14 May 1987.

53. In April 1992, Pathfinder Tours ran 'The Hoovering Druid' railtour from Manchester Piccadilly to Pontycymmer and Ebbw Vale. Here, the special train is seen passing Victoria, between Cwm and Ebbw Vale, as it heads north behind Class 50s 50033 *Glorious* and D400/50050. English Electric Type 3 37212 is on the rear of the train. Ebbw Vale Parkway station was opened in 2008, on the site of the former Victoria station, when passenger services restarted along the line after forty-six years. An extension to a new terminus at Ebbw Vale Town opened in 2015. 4 April 1992.

54. English Electric Type 3 37252 arrives at Ebbw Vale Yard, near the former station of Victoria, with a loaded steel coil train. 14 May 1987.

55. After arriving with a steel coil train, Class 37/9 37901 *Mirrlees Pioneer* shunts its train into Ebbw Vale Yard. 7 April 1987.

56. With the Tinplate and Galvanising Works in the background, Class 60 60029 heads an empty steel train out of the north sidings at Ebbw Vale. The steelworks was the largest steel mill in Europe by the late 1930s. Following nationalisation, iron and steel making was discontinued in the 1970s and the site was redeveloped as a tinplate works. It was closed in 2002. 9 March 1996.

57. Hunslet-Barclay 0-6-0 diesel-hydraulic *Gillian* (6769 of 1990, rebuilt from AB 660 of 1982) heads a steel coil train at Ebbw Vale works. A second locomotive is on the rear of the train. In 1990, three locomotives were hired from Hunslet-Barclay to replace British Steel's earlier 0-8-0 diesel-hydraulics at Ebbw Vale. The other two locomotives were *Laura* (Hunslet-Barclay 6767 of 1990, rebuilt from AB 646 of 1979) and *Tracey* (Hunslet-Barclay 6768 of 1990, rebuilt from AB 659 of 1982). 25 August 1994. (*Paul Dorney Photo*)

58. The freight line to Machen Quarry leaves the Ebbw Vale line at Park Junction, Newport. Here, in Transrail livery, Class 37/7 37896 heads a loaded ballast train, from Machen quarry to Alexandra Dock Junction Yard, past the former Church Road station at Lower Machen. The station closed in 1957. 10 May 1997.

59. Machen Quarry is located on a remaining section of the former Brecon and Merthyr Railway. Here, British Rail Type 5 Co-Co diesel-electric 56031 *Merehead* arrives at the quarry with a train of Amey Roadstone (ARC) aggregate hopper wagons. The quarry now belongs to Hanson Aggregates. 7 April 1987.

Above: **60. Machen Quarry** had its own shunting locomotives. Here, Rolls-Royce Sentinel 0-4-0 diesel-hydraulic 10222 of 1965 passes under the loader as it prepares to shunt wagons at the quarry. On the right is F.C. Hibberd Planet 0-4-0 diesel-hydraulic 3890 of 1959. The Sentinel is now preserved at the Llanelli and Mynydd Mawr Railway and the Planet at the Garw Valley Railway. 7 April 1987.

Opposite above: **61. F.C. Hibberd** Planet chain-driven 0-4-0 diesel-mechanical locomotive 3832 of 1957 is pictured on a low loader at Machen Quarry. The locomotive was on its way to British Industrial Sand Ltd, Redhill, Surrey. It is now preserved at the Bideford Railway Heritage Centre. 6 October 1986.

Opposite below: **62. In May** 1987, Pathfinder Tours ran the 'Gwent Valley Explorer' to Ebbw Vale, Machen, Barry Island and Oakdale using 37280, 37220 and 40122. Here, 37280 runs under the loader at Machen Quarry as the train heads for Cardiff Central and Barry Island. A second Class 37, 37220, is on the rear. 23 May 1987.

NEWPORT TO CARDIFF

63. In Waterman Railways livery, Brush Type 4 47705 *Guy Fawkes* heads along the four-track main line between Newport and Cardiff, near Duffryn, with the 08.33 Manchester Piccadilly to Cardiff Central. The day saw Wales play France at Cardiff in a warm-up match for the Rugby World Cup and brought a number of special workings to Cardiff. On this train, the Class 47/7 was substituting for the expected Class 37. 28 August 1999.

64. Class 37s 37042, 37521, and 37223 head a westbound oil tank train near Duffryn, between Newport and Cardiff. The train will be bound for one of the oil terminals at Milford Haven in South West Wales. 27 February 1993.

AROUND CARDIFF

65. British Rail Type 5 56069 passes the container terminal at Pengam, Cardiff, with an empty coal train from Doncaster to Briton Ferry. In the background, 47705 *Lothian* heads empty stock from Pengam to Cardiff Central in connection with an England vs Wales Five Nations Championship Rugby match at Cardiff Arms Park. 19 January 1991.

66. With the Highland Stag emblem of Inverness TMD on its cab, Brush Type 4 47630 shunts the 4V68 03.50 container train from Holyhead under the overhead crane at the container terminal at Pengam. 2 February 1991.

67. British Rail Type 5 56032 *Sir De Morgannwg/County of South Glamorgan* heads the 6E47 Cardiff Tidal to Scunthorpe loaded steel train onto the Cardiff to Newport main line at Pengam Junction. 6 February 1993.

Above: **68. British Rail** Class 08 0-6-0 diesel-electric shunter 08819 shunts scrap steel wagons at Splott Junction, Cardiff. A second 08 is on the rear of the train. Allied Steel & Wire hired Class 08 shunters from Transrail and later English, Welsh and Scottish Railway for shunting duties at their works. 21 November 1998.

Opposite above: **69. Class 37/9** 37905 approaches Splott Junction at Cardiff with a slag train from Llanwern Steelworks to Cardiff Docks. 28 November 1998.

Opposite below: **70. After visiting** Associated British Ports Cardiff Docks, Class 37/7 diesel-electrics 37894 and 37887 *Castell Caerffili/Caerphilly Castle* arrive at Splott Junction with Hertfordshire Rail Tours' 'The Welsh Rarebit' railtour from Paddington to Cardiff Docks and various other locations in South Wales. Class 47/7 47741 is on the rear of the train. On the right is Allied Steel and Wire 0-6-0 diesel-electric shunter 390, Yorkshire Engine Company 2758 of 1959. Since heavy rain was the order of the day, the staff member arrived from the works in this and used it as a shelter until it was time for token duties. 11 March 1995.

71. Preserved diesel-electric multiple unit 1001, in green livery, heads west near Pengam along the main line from Newport to Cardiff Central. The working is in association with a 1999 Rugby World Cup match at Cardiff's Millennium Stadium. Previously, in regular service, the diesel unit was used on the London Charing Cross to Hastings route. 23 October 1999.

72. Class 37/9 diesel-electrics 37903 and 37904 pass Long Dyke Junction as they head west towards Cardiff Central with iron ore empties from Llanwern to Port Talbot. 31 December 1990.

73. English Electric Type 3 37701 and BRCW Type 3 33101 approach Cardiff Central with the 2Z10 09.56 from Salisbury. The train ran in association with the Rugby Union Five Nations Championship at Cardiff Arms Park where the final score was Wales 10, England 9. Diana, Princess of Wales, attended the match. 6 February 1993.

74. In grey and yellow livery, English Electric Type 3 37263 heads an empty ballast train eastwards under the line from Cardiff Bute Road to Cardiff Queen Street. Cardiff Central station is beyond the bridge. 18 April 1995.

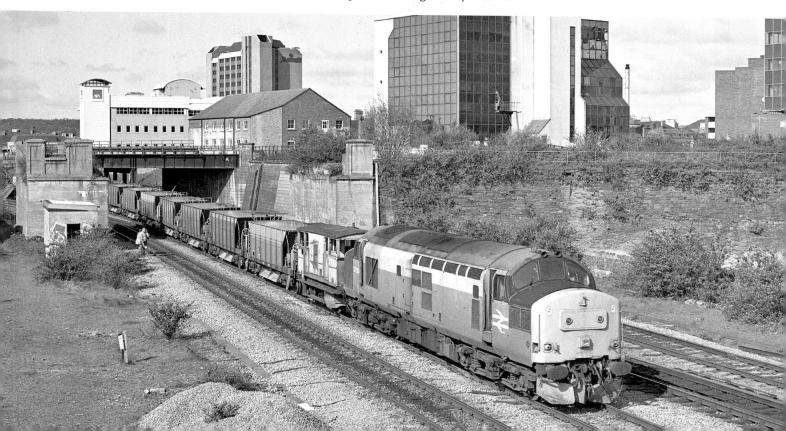

75. In 1987, Hertfordshire Rail Tours ran 'The Valleybasher II' railtour from Finsbury Park to Nantgarw, Cardiff Bute Road, and Cwm Bargoed. Here, the special train stands at Cardiff Bute Road after arriving from Nantgarw behind Class 37/9 37905 *Vulcan Enterprise*. BRCW Type 3 'Cromptons' 33062 and 33025 are on the other end of the train. 28 February 1987.

CARDIFF TO RHYMNEY

76. The Rhymney Line runs from Cardiff Central along the Rhymney valley to Caerphilly, Bargoed and Rhymney. Here, in Regional Railways livery, Class 37/4 37420 *The Scottish Hosteller* departs from Cardiff Queen Street with the 12.50 Cardiff Central to Rhymney. Because of the regular use of Class 37 diesels on passenger trains into the twenty-first century, the line was very popular with railway enthusiasts and photographers. 5 February 2000.

77. In EWS livery, Class 37/4 37413 approaches Cardiff Queen Street with the 10.15 Rhymney to Cardiff Central. 11 November 2000.

78. Painted in BR green livery, 37403 *Ben Cruachan* heads south, between Heath High Level and Cardiff Queen Street, with the 09.15 Rhymney to Cardiff Central. 5 February 2000.

79. English Electric
Type 3 37412 *Driver John Elliott* arrives at Llanishen with the 10.15 Rhymney to Cardiff Central. 5 December 1998.

80. During International Rugby matches at Cardiff's Millennium Stadium, additional trains ran to Cardiff Central, including top and tailed shuttle services on the Rhymney line. A variety of motive power was used on these trains, including privately-owned Class 50 diesel-electrics. Here, 50044, running as D444, departs from Caerphilly with the 12.15 Bargoed to Cardiff Central on the occasion of a Rugby World Cup warm up match at Cardiff. Class 50 50031 *Hood* is on the rear of the train. 21 August 1999.

81. Class 37/5 37505 is pictured during Sunday ballasting operations at Caerphilly. 13 July 1986.

82. F & W Railtours' 'The Red Dragon' ran from Crewe to Aberthaw, Nantgarw, Cwmbargoed and Penarth. Here, English Electric Type 3 37699 passes Aber Junction, north of Caerphilly, with the Cwmbargoed to Cardiff leg of the railtour. Aber Junction signal box was a British Railways (Western Region) Type 14, fitted with a 107 lever frame. It was opened in 1953 and closed in 1987. 11 October 1986.

83. English Electric diesel-electrics 37213 and 37298 pass Aber Junction with an empty coal train from Aberthaw Power Station to Cwmbargoed Coal Disposal Point. 15 July 1986.

84. Aber Junction was the junction of the lines to Rhymney, Caerphilly and Radyr. Here, disused tracks and signals with missing arms are in evidence as Class 116 DMU set C304 passes with a working to Penarth. 16 July 1986.

85. Class 37/4
37414 *Cathays C&W Works 1846-1993* passes the site of Llanbradach Colliery, closed in 1961, as it approaches Llanbradach station with the 09.15 Rhymney to Cardiff Central. Various old colliery buildings still remain. 18 March 2000.

86. British Rail
Class 142 Pacer DMUs 142092 and 142091, forming the 09.06 Bargoed to Cardiff, depart from Llanbradach. The station was opened in 1893 by the Rhymney Railway. 20 May 2000.

87. English Electric Type 3 diesel-electrics 37294 and 37275 approach Ystrad Mynach South Junction with an empty coal train from Aberthaw Power Station to Penallta Colliery. 14 July 1986.

88. English Electric Type 3 diesel-electrics 37294 and 37275 pass Ystrad Mynach South Junction with a loaded coal train from Penallta Colliery to Aberthaw Power Station. The lines to Cwmbargoed, and Rhymney and Penallta Colliery, divide at the South Junction. Ystrad Mynach South signal box was built to a McKenzie & Holland 1875 design. The box opened around 1890 and closed in 2013. 18 July 1986.

89. English Electric Type 3 37505 approaches Ystrad Mynach South Junction with a loaded coal train from the Cwmbargoed line. Ystrad Mynach station is on the right. 14 July 1986.

90. Class 37/4 37414 *Cathays C&W Works 1846-1993* arrives at Ystrad Mynach with the 09.50 Cardiff Central to Rhymney. The Class 37/4 was rebuilt from Class 37/0 37287 in 1985, so it is not clear why the locomotive has 609 written on its nose. The line to Cwmbargoed is on the right. 28 August 1999.

91. Class 37/5 diesel-electrics 37508 and 37511 head a loaded coal train, from Penallta Colliery to Aberthaw Power Station, through Ystrad Mynach. The Class 37/5 locomotives were rebuilt from Class 37/0 locomotives with split headcode boxes. 14 July 1986.

92. Penallta Colliery, near Hengoed and located on the former Cylla freight line, was connected to the Rhymney line at Ystrad Mynach North Junction. The colliery closed in 1991. Here, 37799 waits at Penallta Colliery while its empty coal train from Aberthaw is filled. 28 February 1987.

93. Class 47/7 47711 *County of Hertfordshire* heads away from Hengoed with the 11.32 Cardiff Central to Bargoed. Class 37/4 37416 *Mt Fuji* is on the rear of the train. The train ran in connection with the England vs Wales Five Nations Rugby Championship match at Cardiff. Hengoed Viaduct, in the background, was built to carry the Taff Vale Extension of the Newport, Abergavenny and Hereford Railway across the Rhymney River. It is now a cycle route. 18 February 1995.

94. Class 37/4 37412 *Driver John Elliott* arrives at the small station of Gilfach Fargoed with the 12.40 Bargoed to Penarth. Brush Type 4 47296 is on the rear of the train. The train ran in connection with the Ireland vs Wales Five Nations Rugby Championship match at Cardiff. 18 March 1995.

95. Class 37/4 37407 *Blackpool Tower* approaches Gilfach Fargoed with the 15.15 Rhymney to Cardiff Central. 28 August 1999.

96. Class 37/4 37407 *Blackpool Tower* approaches Bargoed with the 13.50 Cardiff Central to Rhymney. The former Bargoed Colliery, closed in 1977, was located in the area on the left. 21 August 1999.

97. In blue Mainline livery, English Electric Type 3 37371 arrives at Bargoed with the 14.15 Rhymney to Cardiff Central. The station was opened in 1858 by the Rhymney Railway and was once a junction station with lines to Newport and Brecon. 21 August 1999.

98. English Electric Type 3 37402 *Bont Y Bermo* arrives at Bargoed with the 13.15 Rhymney to Cardiff Central. The name, which means Barmouth Bridge, was previously carried by Welsh Class 37/4 37427 and was transferred to this former Scottish locomotive in February 1994. The Western Region signal box was originally at Cymmer Afan and was moved to Bargoed in 1970. 6 April 2002.

99. English Electric
Type 3 37178 departs from Brithdir with the 16.10 Rhymney to Penarth. Brush Type 4 47524 is on the rear of the train. The train ran in connection with the Ireland vs Wales Five Nations Rugby Championship match at Cardiff. 18 March 1995.

100. English Electric
37412 *Driver John Elliott* trails at the rear of the 13.47 Penarth to Rhymney as it arrives at Tirphil station. Brush Type 4 47296 is on the front of the train. 18 March 1995.

101. In 1998, a Class 50 Railtour in South Wales, using 50031 *Hood,* was organised by the Cardiff Railway Company. The company ran the train on Sunday, helping to reduce the loadings on the commuter trains that used the Class 50 on weekdays. The itinerary was 09.55 Rhymney to Treherbert, 12.33 Treherbert to Merthyr Tydfil and 14.38 Merthyr Tydfil to Rhymney. Here, *Hood* approaches Tirphil with the 1Z10 09.55 Rhymney to Treherbert. The special was repeated the following week. 9 August 1998.

102. After crossing Pontlottyn viaduct, 37427, in EWS livery, is nearing the end of its journey as it heads the 11.02 from Cardiff Central towards Rhymney. 29 November 1997.

103. English Electric Type 3 37420 *The Scottish Hosteller* heads south from Pontlottyn with the 14.15 Rhymney to Cardiff Central. 22 April 2000.

104. With enthusiasts looking out of the train's windows and enjoying the sound of the locomotive, 37426 starts away from the Pontlottyn station stop with the 15.15 Rhymney to Cardiff Central. 13 October 2001.

105. In Rail Express Systems livery, 47745 *Royal London Society for the Blind* reaches its destination as it arrives at Rhymney with the 14.47 from Penarth. English Electric Type 3 37141 is on the rear of the train. The train ran in connection with the England vs Wales Five Nations Rugby Championship match at Cardiff. 18 February 1995.

YSTRAD MYNACH TO CWMBARGOED

106. The freight line to Cwmbargoed leaves the Rhymney line at Ystrad Mynach South Junction. Less than a mile to the north of the junction was Nelson Bog colliery spoil tip. Here, 37689 with a train of HAA wagons, which would have originated at either Deep Navigation or Taff Merthyr Colliery, is pictured at the tip. 31 March 1990. (*Paul Dorney Photo*)

107. Class 37/5 37503 departs from Nelson East Sidings at Nelson Bog spoil tip after discharging its load of colliery spoil. 14 July 1986.

108. English Electric Type 3 diesel-electrics 37511 and 37508 arrive at Deep Navigation Colliery with an empty coal train from Aberthaw Power Station. The colliery, located at Treharris on a branch line from Nelson, closed in 1991. 14 July 1986.

109. English Electric Type 3 diesel-electrics 37508 and 37511 are pictured at Deep Navigation Colliery, on the former Vale of Neath line from Neath to Pontypool Road, as their train is loaded with coal for Aberthaw Power Station. In the foreground is Ocean Taff Merthyr Junction, with the line on the right leading to Taff Merthyr Colliery. 14 July 1986.

110. The Growler Group ran 'The Glamorgan Growler' railtour from Wolverhampton to Tower Colliery, Cwmbargoed and Maesteg Llynfi Junction. Here, after visiting Cwmbargoed, 37702 passes Taff Merthyr Colliery as it heads down the valley towards Nelson and Ystrad Mynach. A second Class 37, 37355, is on the rear of the train. 6 May 1989.

111. Pictured north of Trelewis, 37799 *Sir Dyfed/County of Dyfed*, 37704 and 37802 head south with a loaded coal train from Cwmbargoed to Aberthaw Power Station. 21 May 1995.

112. To mark the official end of Class 37-hauled trains in the valleys, a number of special trains were organised using 37038. Here, one of the specials is pictured near Bedlinog as it heads its train from Cwmbargoed to Cardiff. 10 June 2000.

113. In Mainline livery, British Rail Class 58 58015 approaches Bedlinog with a Cwmbargoed to Westbury stone train. The gritstone will be worked forward to Hayes & Harlington. 7 August 1998. (*Paul Dorney Photo*)

114. In Transrail livery, 37701 and 37896 head through Bedlinog with an empty coal train from Aberthaw Power Station to Cwmbargoed Disposal Point. 1 June 1996.

115. Class 37/7 37800 *Glo Cymru* heads a loaded coal train to Aberthaw away from Cwmbargoed. 28 February 1987.

116. Coal mined at Ffos-y-fran is brought to Cwmbargoed Disposal Point for processing and, with most going through the crushing and blending plant, coal for power generation and cement manufacture is produced. Here, 37896 and 37701 wait at Cwmbargoed while their train is loaded, before departing to Aberthaw Power Station. 1 June 1996.

117. A second view of a coal train being loaded at Cwmbargoed. The locomotives are 37797 and 37887 *Castell Caerffili/Caerphilly Castle* on this occasion. 30 April 1995. (*Paul Dorney Photo*)

LLANDAFF TO PONTYPRIDD

118. North of Cardiff Queen Street, the line to Radyr and Pontypridd diverges from the Rhymney Line. Here, Class 118 DMU set C465 approaches Llandaf, between Radyr and Cardiff Queen Street, as it heads for Cardiff. The station was opened by the Taff Vale Railway in 1840 as Llandaff. It was renamed Llandaf in 1980. The Taff Vale Llandaff Loop Junction signal box, dating from 1900, was closed in 1998. The Llandaff Loop Line, on the left, leads to Radyr Yard. 12 July 1986.

119. English Electric Type 3 diesel-electrics 37258 and 37285 approach Llandaf station with a loaded coal train from Lady Windsor Colliery to Aberthaw Power Station. 13 July 1986.

120. After arriving at Llandaf from Treherbert, Class 116 DMU set C314 departs for Cardiff and Barry Island. Only one passenger has left the train on this occasion. 13 July 1986.

121. Passing between some fine semaphore signals, Class 116 DMU set C302 heads for Cardiff as it departs from Radyr. Radyr station, opened as Penarth Junction by the Taff Vale Railway in 1883, was an important railway junction and the location of a freight yard. 13 July 1986.

122. English Electric Type 3 diesel-electrics 37294 and 37275 pass Taffs Well with an empty coal train from Aberthaw Power Station to Lady Windsor Colliery. 15 July 1986.

123. Class 116 DMU set C317 passes Walnut Tree Junction as it departs from Taffs Well towards Cardiff. The former Rhymney Railway main line to Rhymney via Aber Junction, known as the 'Big Hill', is on the right. The line was closed in 1982. The Taff Vale Railway's Walnut Tree Junction signal box, built to a McKenzie and Holland design, closed in early 1997. 13 July 1986.

124. Class 116 DMU set C302, forming a southbound service, arrives at Taffs Well station, opened by the Taff Vale Railway in 1863. Note the centre-pivot signals on the left. The line to Nantgarw Colliery, opened by British Railways in 1952, diverges to the right just behind the train. 15 July 1986.

125. Nantgarw Colliery opened in 1910, with the coke ovens opening in 1951, and was closed in December 1986. Here, after the closure, a line of shunters stands at the coking works. They are, from left to right, 4 (Class 11 12061), 5 (Class 11 12063), 6 (Class 11 12071), and 7 (Hunslet 'Snibstone' Class 0-6-0 diesel-hydraulic 6973 of 1969). The former British Railways Class 11 0-6-0 diesel-electric shunting locomotives were built between 1945 and 1952. The writing on the side of the Hunslet reads 'National Smokeless Fuels, Nantgarw Coking Works'. 28 February 1987.

126. English Electric Type 3 37251 heads south through Pontypridd with a loaded coal train from Maerdy Colliery. Pontypridd station, located at the junction of the Merthyr and Rhondda lines, was opened by the Taff Vale Railway in 1840. 5 July 1986.

127. Class 143 Pacer 143 604, forming a Merthyr Tydfil to Barry Island service, approaches Pontypridd. The Rhondda line, on the left, runs to Treherbert. Pontypridd Junction signal box is a modified McKenzie and Holland Type 3 design built in 1902. The box closed in 1988. 12 September 1999.

PONTYPRIDD TO MERTHYR TYDFIL

128. Lady Windsor Colliery was located at the end of a freight line from Stormstown Junction, south of Abercynon. The colliery, in the village of Ynysybwl, opened in 1884. It was closed in 1988, more than 100 years later. Here, after arriving at the loading point, 37294 and 37284 prepare to run round their train prior to loading. 29 May 1986. (*Paul Dorney Photo*)

129. Abercynon station, opened in 1840, is located at the junction of the lines to Pontypridd, Merthyr Tydfil, and Tower Colliery via Aberdare. During a busy period, 37427 *Bont Y Bermo* passes with a coal train to Abercwmboi Phurnacite Plant, while 37239 waits next to the GWR signal box with an empty coal train to Merthyr Vale Colliery. 15 July 1986.

130. English Electric Type 3 37233 accelerates away from Abercynon with an additional southbound working from the Aberdare line. The GWR Type 27c signal box, previously located at Birmingham Moor Street and Didcot Foxhall Junction, was moved to Abercynon in 1932. The box closed in 2008 and was demolished in 2013. The old steam shed is on the right. 13 July 1986.

131. Opened as Quakers Yard Low Level by the Taff Vale Railway in 1858, Quakers Yard station, on the line to Merthyr Tydfil, serves the village of Edwardsville. Here, Class 117 DMU set T305, forming a Taff Vale Railway 150th Anniversary special working from Cardiff Bute Road to Merthyr Tydfil, pauses at the station. The DMU is painted in GWR chocolate and cream livery. 23 June 1991.

132. Class 150 Sprinter 150 271, forming the 13.41 Penarth to Merthyr Tydfil, heads away from Black Lion signal box near Merthyr Vale. The British Railways (Western Region) Type 37 signal box was moved from Cynheidre and opened in 1971. It was closed in 1992. 23 June 1991.

133. English Electric Type 3 37239 shunts its coal train in the exchange sidings at Merthyr Vale Colliery, near Black Lion. Note the former British Railways shunter in the background. 15 July 1986.

134. Class 116 DMU set C335, forming a Merthyr Tydfil to Cardiff Central service, passes Merthyr Vale Colliery. It was the collapse of a spoil tip from this colliery that was responsible for the Aberfan disaster in October 1966. The colliery closed in 1989. 15 July 1986.

135. Split-box Class 37/0 37038 heads a special train from Cardiff to Merthyr Tydfil, between Pentre-bach and Merthyr Tydfil, in connection with Cardiff Cathays' Festival of Transport. 4 June 2000.

ABERCYNON TO TOWER COLLIERY

136. Running northwest from Abercynon is the line to Aberdare and Tower Colliery. Abercwmboi Phurnacite Plant was located north of Mountain Ash. Here, 0-6-0 diesel-electric 08375 shunts coal wagons at the plant. The plant, which produced smokeless fuel for fifty years, was closed in 1991. The Taff Vale Railway signal box, opened in 1884, was closed in 1989. 17 July 1986.

137. The Growler Group's 'The Glamorgan Growler' railtour from Wolverhampton crosses the Afon Cynon at Cwmbach as it heads to Tower Colliery behind 37355. Class 37/7 37702 is on the rear of the train. The girder bridge over the river, which replaced an earlier bridge, was recovered from Wheatley on the Kennington Junction to Princes Risborough line. The siding with a buffer stop in the background was once part of the closed section of the Taff Vale Railway. Some sidings associated with Abercwmboi Phurnacite Plant were also in the area. 6 May 1989.

138. After visiting Tower Colliery, 37702 heads 'The Glamorgan Growler' through Aberdare station, closed in 1964. A second Class 37, 37355, is on the rear of the train. Passenger services returned to Aberdare in 1988. 6 May 1989.

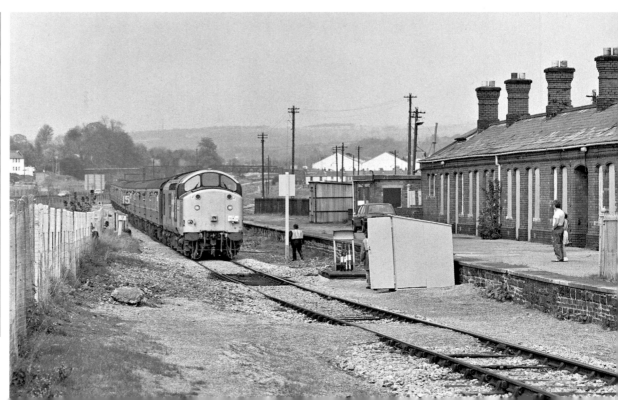

139. With 37355 on the rear of the train, Class 37/7 37702 is pictured at Hirwaun with 'The Glamorgan Growler' railtour from Wolverhampton. 6 May 1989.

140. British Rail Type 5 56114 *Maltby Colliery* heads a loaded coal train to Aberthaw Power Station away from Tower Colliery. The colliery, located near the village of Hirwaun, closed in 2008. 25 August 1994. (*Paul Dorney Photo*)

141. British Rail Type 5 56044 *Cardiff Canton Quality Assured* waits at Tower Colliery while its train, the 7Z01 09.46 to Aberthaw Power Station, is loaded with coal. 30 June 1994. (*Steve Turner Photo*)

PONTYPRIDD TO TREHERBERT

142. The Rhondda Valley line runs northwest from Pontypridd to Treherbert, with a branch from Porth to Maerdy Colliery. Here, Class 37/0 37251 heads away from Porth towards Pontypridd with a coal train from Maerdy Colliery. 15 July 1986.

143. English Electric Type 3 37251 takes the line to Maerdy Colliery at Porth with coal empties from Abercwmboi Phurnacite Plant. The final closure of the branch to the colliery took place in August 1986. 15 July 1986.

144. Running next to the Rhondda River, 50031 *Hood* heads the 1Z11 12.33 Treherbert to Merthyr Tydfil south from Dinas. The special train was organised by the Cardiff Railway Company and was a repeat of one of a series of special trains which ran the previous Sunday. 16 August 1998.

145. Privately-owned Class 50, 50031 *Hood,* heads the 1Z11 12.33 Treherbert to Merthyr Tydfil between Ton Pentre and Ystrad Rhondda. The train was organised by the Cardiff Railway Company. 9 August 1998.

146. Class 150 Sprinter 150 279, forming a service to Treherbert, departs from Ton Pentre station as it heads north towards its destination. 4 June 2000.

PORTH TO MAERDY

Above: **147. English** Electric Type 3 37251 heads a loaded coal train to Abercwmboi Phurnacite Plant away from Maerdy Colliery. 15 July 1986.

Opposite above: **148.** Maerdy Colliery, in the Rhondda Valley, opened in 1875 and closed in 1990. From 30 June 1986, coal from the colliery was raised at Tower Colliery. Here, just over two weeks before rail traffic ceased, 37251 heads a loaded coal train to Abercwmboi out of the colliery sidings. 15 July 1986.

Opposite below: **149.** Two weeks before the end of coal traffic on the Maerdy line, Class 37/5 37503 stands in the sidings at Maerdy Colliery with an empty coal train from Radyr. 17 July 1986.

CARDIFF TO BRIDGEND, THE MAIN LINE

Above: **150. To the** west of Cardiff Central, on the south side of the line to Bridgend and South West Wales, is Cardiff Canton TMD. Here, 60035 *Florence Nightingale* passes the depot with an empty iron ore train from Llanwern Steelworks to Port Talbot. 29 December 1994.

Opposite above: **151. British Rail** Type 5 56113 passes Cardiff Canton as it heads towards Cardiff Central with a loaded steel train. 29 December 1994.

Opposite below: **152. Cardiff Canton** depot was built in 1882 as a six-road shed by the South Wales Railway. Various additions and modifications were made to the depot by the GWR and around 120 locomotives were allocated there during its peak. Steam traction at the depot ended in September 1962 and a new facility for diesel traction was built, opening in 1964. Here, 37797 and 37668 stand next to the old water tower at Cardiff Canton TMD. Class 08 shunters 08652 and 08848 are in the background. 20 February 1993.

153. Class 108 DMU set S942, forming a Llandovery to Cardiff Central service, passes Cardiff Canton TMD as it nears the end of its journey. On the right, an InterCity 125 unit, forming a Swansea to London Paddington service, slowly approaches the signal as it waits for the road into the station. 31 December 1990.

154. The 'Class 58 Farewell' railtour, organised by Worksop Depot CTC, ran from Worksop to Swansea Burrows Sidings and Tondu. Here, British Rail Class 58 diesel-electrics 58037 *Worksop Depot* and 58024, in EWS livery, cross the River Ely at Miskin with the returning special. Class 60 60070 is on the rear of the train. 1 July 2000.

155. An unidentified InterCity 125 unit, forming a London Paddington to Swansea service, approaches Llantrisant Ely Valley Junction as it heads west towards Bridgend. 6 May 1989.

156. British Rail Class 143 Pacer 143 621, forming the 13.15 Maesteg to Cardiff Central service, departs from Pontyclun station. The station, previously called Llantrisant, closed in 1964. It was rebuilt and reopened by British Rail as Pontyclun in 1992. What was Llantrisant Ely Valley Junction but is now the junction of the line to Llantrisant Sidings can be seen just beyond the station. 18 April 1995.

157. With power car 43188 leading, the InterCity 125 unit, forming the 11.10 Swansea to London Paddington service, waits for departure time at Bridgend. The station, opened in 1850, is located on the main line from Cardiff to Swansea at the junction of the line to Maesteg and the Vale of Glamorgan line from Cardiff. 19 August 1990.

CARDIFF TO BARRY ISLAND

158. Having run from Bridgend via the Vale of Glamorgan line, the InterCity 125 unit forming the diverted 10.40 Swansea to London Paddington heads east from Cadoxton towards Cardiff. Power car 43040 is leading. 23 April 1995.

159. With Barry Docks in the background, British Rail Type 5 56064 runs through Cadoxton station with the Barry Docks to Burn Naze vinyl chloride monomer tanks. 15 March 1997.

160. Hertfordshire Rail Tours' 'The Welsh Rarebit' railtour ran from London Paddington to Cardiff Docks, Barry Docks, Cwmgwrach and Baglan Bay. Here, the railtour pauses at Associated British Ports Barry Docks behind 37887 *Castell Caerffili/Caerphilly Castle* and 37894. Brush Type 4 47741 *Resilient* is on the rear of the train. Opened in 1889, the area around the first dock has now been redeveloped for residential and commercial use. The second dock is still active. 11 March 1995.

161. 'The Welsh Rarebit' railtour passes the cranes at Barry Docks No. 2 dock behind 37894 and 37887 *Castell Caerffili/Caerphilly Castle*. Brush Type 4 47741 *Resilient* is on the rear of the train. 11 March 1995.

162. Class 116 DMU set C331, forming a service to Barry Island, approaches Barry station. Barry signal box is a Barry Railway Type 1 design, dating from around 1897. It was originally fitted with a 117-lever Evans, O'Donnell frame, replaced in 1957 by a GWR frame. 13 July 1985.

163. After travelling along the Vale of Glamorgan line from Bridgend, British Rail Type 5 60062 *Samuel Johnson* approaches Barry station as it heads east with a steel coil train. Opened in 1889, Barry is the junction of the lines to Cardiff, Barry Island and the Vale of Glamorgan Line to Bridgend. The line to Barry Island curves away to the left. 23 April 1995.

164. The railway line to Barry Island station, opened in 1896, was built along the road causeway from Barry. Here, Class 116 DMU set C320, forming a Treherbert to Barry Island service, arrives at the station. Barry Island signal box is a McKenzie and Holland design, moved from Nantgarw in 1929. It was rebuilt in 1976 after suffering fire damage. The box closed in 1998. 13 July 1985.

165. Class 116 DMU set C304 waits for departure time at Barry Island. The station is located at the end of the branch line from Barry. The railway previously continued to Barry Pier station, closed in 1976. 13 July 1985.

166. Pathfinder Tours' 'The Gwent Valley Explorer' visited Barry Island in May 1987. Here, the railtour is pictured at Barry Island after arriving from Machen Quarry behind English Electric Type 3 37280. 23 May 1987.

BARRY SCRAPYARD

Above: **167. The scrapyard** of Woodham Brothers Ltd, located in the disused sidings associated with Barry Docks, disposed of former British Railways' equipment, including locomotives and wagons. Priority was given to coal wagons from the South Wales coalfield and, as a result, the majority of the locomotives remained in the yard for many years. A total of eighty-seven locomotives were scrapped, including four diesels, while the remainder, all steam locomotives, were purchased by preservationists. The deteriorating state of the steam locomotives, after twenty years or more in the sea air, can be seen here. 13 July 1985.

Opposite above: **168. Lines of** derelict locomotives stand at Barry Scrapyard in 1985. On the left is a rebuilt Bulleid Pacific, and at the front of the line on the right is a GWR 2-8-0. Perhaps the smiling face on the smokebox door means that the locomotive has already been acquired for preservation. I found it very interesting to walk among the locomotives to look at what had happened with their preservation since my previous visit. 13 July 1985.

Opposite below: **169. Locomotives acquired** for preservation stand at Barry Scrapyard. Prominent is Bulleid Pacific 34081 *92 Squadron*. Other locomotives present include a GWR tank engine, a rebuilt Bulleid Pacific, a Hughes Crab 2-6-0, and a Modified Hall 4-6-0. A total of 213 steam locomotives were saved from the scrapyard, many of which have been restored. Some have been cannibalised for parts for other locomotives, while others still remain in scrapyard condition. 28 September 1974.

170. Four diesels were scrapped at Barry, D600 *Active*, D601 *Ark Royal*, D6122, and D8206. Here, A1A-A1A diesel-hydraulic D601 *Ark Royal* stands at Barry Scrapyard next to a rebuilt Bulleid Pacific. Built by the North British Locomotive Company in 1958 and withdrawn in 1967, the locomotive was unfortunately scrapped in July 1980. Diesel preservation had not really taken off in those days and it was considered to be too far gone to be restored to operational condition. 1 Feb 1976.

BARRY TO BRIDGEND, THE VALE OF GLAMORGAN LINE

171. Class 37/7 diesel-electrics 37799 *Sir Dyfed/County of Dyfed*, 37704, and 37802 head a coal train, from Cwmbargoed to Aberthaw Power Station, through Barry station and onto the Vale of Glamorgan Line. The line curving away to the right leads to Barry Island. 21 May 1995.

172. An unidentified Class 37 crosses Porthkerry Viaduct, between Barry and Rhoose, with a coal train to Aberthaw Power Station. The sixteen-arch viaduct was originally opened in 1897, but stability problems meant that repairs were required. It reopened in January 1900. 5 May 1993. (*Paul Dorney Photo*)

173. English Electric Type 3 diesel-electrics 37799 *Sir Dyfed/County of Dyfed*, 37704, and 37802 approach Aberthaw with a coal train from Cwmbargoed to the power station. 21 May 1995.

174. Passing a pair of semaphore signals, English Electric Type 3 37146 heads an eastbound ballast train away from Aberthaw. Aberthaw Cement Works is in the background. 21 May 1995.

175. Diverted from the main line because of Sunday engineering work, an InterCity 125 unit, forming the 14.25 Swansea to London Paddington, passes Aberthaw. A loaded coal train for Aberthaw Power Station is on the left. A Barry Railway Type 2 signal box, opened in 1897, stands on the platform of the former Aberthaw High Level station. 23 April 1995.

TONDU AND ITS BRANCHES

Above: **176. Class 37/7** 37894 arrives at Tondu with a coal train from Pontycymer. The station, opened in 1864, was originally the junction of the railways from Porthcawl to Maesteg and Abergwynfi, the Maesteg Line to Bridgend, the Ogmore Valley Railway, the Port Talbot Railway, and the Garw Valley Railway to Blaengarw. The station closed in 1970 and reopened in 1992. 18 May 1996.

Opposite Above: **177. Monmouthshire Railway** Society's 'The Cynheidre Curler' ran from Newport using Class 117 DMUs sets L402 and L414. The train visited various destinations in South Wales and is seen here at Ogmore Vale Washery. The washery, opened in 1955, served the collieries in the Ogmore and Llynfi Valleys. It closed in June 1986. 25 October 1986.

Opposite below: **178. Monmouthshire Railway** Society's 'The Cynheidre Curler' reversed at Caedu level crossing on the Ogmore Vale line. Here, the train, with Class 117 DMU set L414 leading, is pictured at the crossing before returning to Tondu and Newport. 25 October 1986.

179. Semaphore signals still remain as can be seen in this second view, looking north, of Caedu level crossing on the A4061. The signal box, opened in 1911, remained until the railway closed in 1987. The barriers replaced the crossing gates in 1977. 16 July 1986.

180. With Class 117 DMU set L402 leading, Monmouthshire Railway Society's 'The Cynheidre Curler' waits while the gates are opened at Brynmenyn level crossing on the A4065 Abergarw Road. The railtour is returning to Tondu from Pontycymer. 25 October 1986.

181. Class 37/7
37894 passes Pontyrhyl as it heads a loaded coal train from Pontycymer to Aberthaw Power Station. 18 May 1996.

182. Class 37/7
37894 stands at Pontycymer while reclaimed coal from the closed Blaengarw Colliery is loaded into its train. 18 May 1996.

183. English Electric Type 3 37254 heads a loaded coal train from Maesteg to Abercwmboi Phurnacite Plant at Maesteg, Llynfi Junction. The locomotive will run round its train before heading south. Note the boarded-up signal box on the right. 16 July 1986.

184. Class 37/7 37887 *Castell Caerffili/Caerphilly Castle* heads a loaded coal train away from Maesteg, Llynfi Junction. 30 September 1992.

185. English Electric Type 3 37220 approaches Tondu with a coal train from Maesteg to Cardiff Tidal Dock. The signal box, formerly Tondu Middle, is a GWR Type 3 design, dating from 1884. 16 July 1986.

BRIDGEND TO SWANSEA

186. Class 37/7 diesel-electrics 37799 *Sir Dyfed/County of Dyfed* and 37704 head east near Laleston, west of Bridgend, with a loaded coal train from Cwmgwrach to Aberthaw Power Station. 11 May 1996.

187. Class 66 Co-Co diesel-electric 66091 approaches Margam Knuckle Yard with a train of imported coal from Grange Coal Terminal. Port Talbot Steelworks is in the background. Opened as Abbey Steelworks in 1951, the works was nationalised in 1967. It was later acquired by the Corus Group, becoming part of Tata Steel Europe by 2010. Today, it is known as Tata Steel Strip Products UK, Port Talbot Works. 12 May 1999. (*Rob Pritchard Photo*)

188. Port Talbot Steelworks has a large internal railway system, with trains frequently moving between the works and the adjacent Margam Knuckle Yard. Here, one of the works shunters, Bo-Bo diesel-electric 902, stands at the entrance to the yard. The locomotive was built by Brush Bagnall Traction Ltd in 1955, works number 3064. 12 May 1999. (*Rob Pritchard Photo*)

189. Brush Type 4 47462 *Cambridge Traction & Rolling Stock Depot* stands at Port Talbot Parkway with a Swansea to Cardiff Central extra for a Wales vs Ireland Five Nations Championship rugby match at Cardiff. Opened in 1850, Port Talbot station was renamed Port Talbot Parkway in 1984. 16 February 1991.

190. English Electric Type 3 diesel-electrics 37097 and 37407 *Blackpool Tower* head east past Briton Ferry Yard with RT Railtours' 'The Sugar Loaf' from Leeds to the Central Wales line. 25 October 1997.

191. Pathfinder Tours' 'The Glamorgan Freighter' ran from Birmingham New Street to various destinations in South Wales. Here, the railtour takes the freight line to Baglan Bay from Briton Ferry Yard behind 37895. Class 37/4 37412 *Driver John Elliott* is on the rear of the train. 2 March 1996.

192. With power car 43010 *TSW Today* leading, the InterCity 125 unit forming the 13.00 London Paddington to Swansea passes Briton Ferry Yard, between Port Talbot and Neath. 16 February 1991.

193. Class 108 DMU set S941, forming the 11.16 Pembroke Dock to Swansea, approaches its destination after rounding the curve from Swansea Loop West Junction. 16 February 1991.

AROUND SWANSEA

194. After passing Jersey Marine South Junction, British Rail Type 5 56093 *The Institution of Mining Engineers* heads for Swansea Burrows Sidings with two Cargowagons. 18 May 1996.

195. After running round their train at Swansea Burrows Sidings, Class 37/7 diesel-electrics 37899 and 37889 head towards Jersey Marine South Junction with a loaded coal train to Aberthaw Power Station. 18 May 1996.

196. English Electric Type 3 37213 waits at Swansea Burrows Sidings with a coal train to Swansea Docks. Class 08 shunter 08191 is on the right. 26 August 1987.

197. Class 37/0 37213 heads its coal train away from Swansea Burrows Sidings towards Swansea Docks. 26 August 1987.

198. Viewed from the Fabian Way road bridge, 37696 heads a coal train from Pantyffynnon out of Swansea Burrows Sidings towards Swansea Docks. The GWR signal box was built in 1910, replacing an earlier box. It was closed in December 1990. 26 August 1987.

199. Looking south from Fabian Way road bridge, 0-6-0 diesel-electric 08191 shunts coal wagons at Swansea Docks. 26 August 1987.

200. Class 37/7 37796 heads a train of empty Kelly's coal containers to Coedbach out of Swansea Docks. Coal was transported by rail from Coedbach Washery and exported to Ireland. King's Dock Junction signal box was a McKenzie and Holland Type 3 design, opened in 1905. It was closed in May 1987. 6 August 1987.

201. Pathfinder Tours' 'The Heart of Wales Excursion' ran from Crewe to Llandrindod Wells. Here, the special passes Llandarcy Siding signal box behind 37029 as it heads for the Central Wales Line. BP Llandarcy refinery, closed in 1998, is in the background. 23 July 2000. (*Paul Dorney Photo*)

NEATH & BRECON JUNCTION TO ONLLWYN AND CWMGWRACH

202. Class 37/7 diesel-electrics 37894 and 37887 *Castell Caerffili/Caerphilly Castle* pass the former Neath Riverside station, closed in 1964, with Hertfordshire Rail Tours' 'The Welsh Rarebit' railtour returning from Cwmgwrach. Brush Type 4 47741 *Resilient* is on the rear of the train. The Neath and Brecon Junction signal box, on the platform, is a GWR Type 5 design, built in 1892. The South Wales main line runs over the bridge at the end of the platform. 11 March 1995.

203. Returning from Onllwyn Washery, Pathfinder Tours' 'The Vulcan Valley Venturer' from Liverpool Lime Street approaches Neath & Brecon Junction behind 37138. English Electric Type 1 diesel-electrics 20106 and 20113 are on the rear of the train. The freight lines to Onllwyn, Cwmgwrach, and Swansea Burrows Sidings joined at the junction. 28 July 1991.

204. Hertfordshire Rail Tours' 'The Welsh Rarebit' railtour, returning from Cwmgwrach, passes Aberdulais behind 37894 and 37887 *Castell Caerffili/Caerphilly Castle*. Brush Type 4 47741 *Resilient* is on the rear of the train. 11 March 1995.

205. Class 37 diesel-electrics 37704 and 37799 *Sir Dyfed/ County of Dyfed* head south at Aberdulais with a coal train from Cwmgwrach to Aberthaw Power Station. 11 May 1996.

206. Class 37/7 diesel-electrics 37799 *Sir Dyfed/ County of Dyfed* and 37704 head an empty coal train from Aberthaw Power Station to Cwmgwrach through Resolven. Resolven station, on the Vale of Neath Railway, was closed in 1964. 11 May 1996.

207. Class 37/7 diesel-electrics 37704 and 37799 *Sir Dyfed/County of Dyfed* wait at Cwmgwrach Washery while their train is loaded with coal for Aberthaw Power Station. The former Vale of Neath Line, which previously ran to Ynysarwed and Aberpergwm Collieries, can be seen on the left. 11 May 1996.

208. Hertfordshire Railtours' 'Route 66' railtour ran from London Paddington to Onllwyn Washery and Cwmgwrach. It was advertised as the first passenger train to be hauled by a Class 66 locomotive. After visiting Onllwyn, the train is seen running down the Dulais Valley, past Cefn Coed colliery museum near Crynant, behind 66011. A second Class 66, 66009, is on the rear of the train. Final clearance of the unwanted colliery infrastructure is taking place in the background. 28 November 1998.

209. Pathfinder Tours' 'The Valley Voyager' ran from Sheffield to Cwmgwrach and Onllwyn. Here, 66145 trails at the rear of the train as the railtour passes Cefn Coed colliery museum behind 37038 and 37197. Coal production at the colliery ended in 1968, but the shafts were kept open to allow access to Blaenant Drift Mine at the same site. Blaenant Drift closed in 1990. 16 March 2002.

210. English Electric Type 3 37241 shunts loaded wagons at Onllwyn Washery. Located in the upper Dulais Valley, the washery was built in 1932 to service local mines. 17 July 1986.

211. English Electric 0-6-0 diesel-hydraulic MP202 (D1230 of 1969) shunts coal wagons at Onllwyn Washery. The locomotive is fitted with a Cummins NT400 engine producing 350 hp. 28 January 1994. (*Paul Dorney Photo*)

THE CENTRAL WALES LINE FROM PANTYFFYNNON TO KNIGHTON INCLUDING FREIGHT LINES AROUND PANTYFFYNNON

212. Class 101 DMU set S805, forming the 06.20 Shrewsbury to Swansea service, pauses at Pantyffynnon station. The station was opened in 1841, and from 1931 a locomotive shed was located there. 26 August 1987.

213. Heading south from Llandrindod Wells, 37097 and 37407 *Blackpool Tower* pass Pantyffynnon with RT Railtours' 'The Sugar Loaf' from Leeds. 25 October 1997.

214. British Rail Class 08 diesel-electric shunter 08798 runs through Pantyffynnon station with a trip working to Wernos Washery. A second Class 08, 08898, is on the rear of the train. The GWR Type 5 signal box, dating from 1892, controls the line north from here to Craven Arms using a system called 'No Signalman Token Remote'. 26 August 1987.

215. With 08798 on the front, British Rail Class 08 diesel-electric shunter 08898 trails at the rear of a trip working to Wernos Washery as it heads away from Pantyffynnon station. The branch line to the washery left the Central Wales Line just to the north of the station. 26 August 1987.

216. From Pantyffynnon, a freight line ran to Gwaun-Cae-Gurwen, with branches to Betws Drift Mine and Abernant. Here, British Rail Class 08 diesel-electric 08898 arrives at Pantyffynnon with a train from Betws Drift Mine near Ammanford. The mine, closed in 2003, was associated with a washery around half a mile to the northeast. 26 August 1987.

217. Viewed from the Pontamman Road bridge, 37800 *Glo Cymru* crosses the River Amman at Ammanford with coal from Gwaun-Cae-Gurwen Colliery. 26 August 1987.

218. Pathfinder Tours' 'The Cymric Gallivant' from Watford Junction passes Glanamman Station signal box, as it heads for Gwaun-Cae-Gurwen, behind 37013 and 37106. Class 37/7 37797 is on the rear of the train. The GWR Type 7 signal box was later used as the meeting place of the Amman Valley Railway Society. 15 April 1995.

219. Class 37/7 37896 heads the 8Z10 12.30 to Llandeilo Junction rail recovery train away from the work-site on the Abernant branch with 37902 on the rear. Just beyond 37902 all the track has been lifted on the branch. The work-site is the Gwaun-Cae-Gurwen station, built but never opened, on the line to Abernant Colliery. There was another Gwaun-Cae-Gurwen station on the line to Gwaun-Cae-Gurwen Colliery. 10 February 1995. (*Steve Turner Photo*)

220. F & W Railtours' 'The Valley Trekker' ran from Plymouth to Abernant, Gwaun-Cae-Gurwen, Cynheidre and Tondu. Here, 37306 passes Cwmgorse station, built but never opened, as the train heads north towards Cwmgorse Branch Junction from Abernant with 25325 and 33012 on the rear. The GWR line was intended to be a through route to Felin Fran but was never completed. 30 November 1985.

221. F & W Railtours' 'The Valley Trekker' from Plymouth stands at Abernant Colliery exchange sidings behind Sulzer Type 2 25325 and BRCW Type 3 33012. English Electric Type 3 37306 is on the rear of the train. Abernant Colliery closed in 1988 but the washery remained open until 1992. 30 November 1985. (*Paul Dorney Photo*)

222. Having just passed Cwmgorse Branch Junction, the crew of the Sulzer Type 2 prepare to open the level crossing gates at Gwaun-Cae-Gurwen, as F & W Railtours' 'The Valley Trekker' from Plymouth slowly approaches behind 25325 and 33012. The four-arch viaduct, on the left, was built to carry an east curve from the existing line and provide a direct route from Gwaun-Cae-Gurwen to Felin Fran by completing a triangular junction. However, the triangle was not completed and the viaduct remained unused. 30 November 1985.

223. English Electric Type 3 37800 *Glo Cymru* heads a coal train across the level crossing on Heol-Cae-Gurwen as it approaches Gwaun-Cae-Gurwen Colliery exchange sidings. The former Gwaun-Cae-Gurwen station was located just beyond the level crossing. 26 August 1987.

224. Class 37/7 37800 *Glo Cymru* heads a loaded coal train out of Gwaun-Cae-Gurwen Colliery exchange sidings. 26 August 1987.

225. An RMS Locotec Class 08 diesel-electric shunts at Gwaun-Cae-Gurwen Colliery exchange sidings. The locomotive is former British Rail 08598. 27 October 1995. (*Paul Dorney Photo*)

226. Powell Duffryn 500hp 0-6-0 diesel-hydraulic 823391 (GEC Traction 5391 of 1973) shunts coal wagons at Gwaun-Cae-Gurwen. 28 January 1994. (*Paul Dorney Photo*)

227. Diesel-hydraulic shunter 823391, owned by Powell Duffryn Coal Preparation Ltd, shunts at Powell Duffryn's Gwaun-Cae-Gurwen Colliery. 28 January 1994. (*Paul Dorney Photo*)

228. Class 37/7 37800 *Glo Cymru* approaches Ammanford with a coal train to Gwaun-Cae-Gurwen. Originally named Duffryn, Ammanford station opened in 1841 as a temporary terminus of the Llanelly Railway's line to Llandeilo. The GWR Type 6 signal box dates from around 1893. 26 August 1987.

229. Metro-Cammell Class 101 DMU set C814, forming the 15.08 Swansea to Shrewsbury service, passes the semaphore signals to the south of Llandeilo as it approaches the station. 31 March 1986.

230. Class 101 DMU set C814, forming the 15.08 Swansea to Shrewsbury service, waits at Llandeilo station for a southbound excursion train to pass. The station was previously named 'Llandilo Junction for the Carmarthen Line'. The GWR Type 15 signal box was opened in 1955. The station building has since been demolished. 31 March 1986.

231. Diverted from its usual route, English Electric Type 3 37521 crosses the River Towy, south of Llandovery, with the 6Z92 05.40 Llanwern Exchange Sidings to Margam Knuckle Yard steel coils. 27 May 1996. (*Steve Turner Photo*)

232. English Electric Type 3 37207 approaches Llandovery with the diverted 6Z93 10.38 Margam Knuckle Yard to Llanwern Exchange Sidings steel coils. 27 May 1996. (*Steve Turner Photo*)

233. Class 101 DMU set C814, forming the 10.50 Shrewsbury to Swansea service, departs from Llandovery. The station was opened by the Vale of Towy Railway Company in 1858. Semaphore signals, as well as much of the old railway infrastructure, are still present. 31 March 1986.

234. Class 101 DMU set C814, forming the 10.50 Shrewsbury to Swansea service, passes the signal box at Tywi Avenue level crossing as it arrives at Llandovery. The former LNWR Llandovery No. 1 signal box was closed in 1986 and became Llandovery Ground Frame. It has since been demolished. 31 March 1986.

235. English Electric Type 3 diesel-electrics 37097 and 37407 *Blackpool Tower* are pictured heading south near Sugar Loaf summit (820ft above sea level) as they approach Sugar Loaf tunnel with RT Railtours' 'The Sugar Loaf' from Leeds to the Central Wales Line. 25 October 1997.

236. With snow on the ground, English Electric Type 3 37214 passes Sugar Loaf station with the 7L59 Llandrindod Wells to Llandeilo Junction empty ballast train. 25 February 1996. (*Steve Turner Photo*)

237. Metro-Cammell Class 101 DMU set C802, forming the 12.30 Swansea to Shrewsbury service, arrives at Llanwrtyd Wells, between Sugar Loaf and Llangammarch. 31 March 1986.

238. Class 101 DMU set C803, forming the 10.10 Swansea to Shrewsbury service, waits to depart from Llanwrtyd Wells. The station was opened by the London and North Western Railway (LNWR) in 1867. 31 March 1986.

239. Class 101 DMU set C803, forming the 10.10 Swansea to Shrewsbury, passes Llanwrtyd Wells signal box as it heads away from the station. The box is an LNWR design, dating from the late nineteenth century, fitted with a non-standard porch. It was closed in 1986 when the line was re-signalled. 31 March 1986.

240. Diverted from their usual route because of Sunday engineering work, Class 37/4 diesel-electrics 37401 *Mary Queen of Scots* and 37426 pass the small station of Cilmeri, between Garth and Builth Road, with the Margam to Dee Marsh steel coils. 28 May 2000.

241. English Electric Type 3 37214 is on ballasting duty at Crossway, south of Llandrindod Wells. The working is the 7L59 07.00 from Llandeilo Junction. 25 February 1996. (*Steve Turner Photo*)

242. In May 1993, British Railways Standard Class 4 2-6-4T 80079 headed a special train from Shrewsbury to Carmarthen. The return journey to Shrewsbury was behind 37414 *Cathays C&W Works 1846-1993*. Here, the Class 37/4 stands at Llandrindod Wells with 80079's support coach before proceeding to Carmarthen. 16 May 1993.

243. Class 150 Sprinter 150 270, forming a Swansea to Shrewsbury service, passes the LNWR Type 4 signal box on the platform, as it arrives at Llandrindod Wells. The box, dating from 1876, is a Grade II listed building and was relocated from its original site at the level crossing to the north of the station in September 1989. It is now a museum. 16 May 1993.

244. The signalman waits as Class 120 DMU set C616, forming the 05.40 Swansea to Shrewsbury service, approaches Llandrindod Wells signal box at Brookland Road level crossing. The box was later preserved at Llandrindod Wells station. 19 April 1986.

245. English Electric Type 3 37521 heads the diverted 6Z92 05.40 Llanwern Exchange Sidings to Margam Knuckle Yard past Llanbister Road station, between Dolau and Llangynllo. The former station building is now a private residence. 27 May 1996. (*Steve Turner Photo*)

246. A Class 101 DMU, forming the 10.10 Swansea to Shrewsbury service, crosses Knucklas Viaduct as it heads towards Knucklas station. The thirteen-arch, castellated viaduct, built in 1866, is a Grade II listed structure spanning the Heyope Valley. 19 April 1986.

247. Metro-Cammell Class 101 DMU set C803, forming the 10.50 Shrewsbury to Swansea service, heads away from the Knighton station stop towards Knucklas. 19 April 1986.

248. A group of passengers wait on the platform as Class 101 DMU set C803, forming the 10.50 Shrewsbury to Swansea service, arrives at Knighton. The station, built in 1865, serves the town of Knighton in Powys, Wales, although the station itself is actually just in England. 19 April 1986.

249. On a dark and rainy day, the appropriately named 'Knighton Horse' railtour stands at Knighton station behind 50007 *Sir Edward Elgar* and D400 (50050) before departing for Shrewsbury. The special train was organised by Pathfinder Tours and ran from Manchester Piccadilly to the Central Wales Line. The passing loop, removed in 1964, was reinstated in 1990, after the modernisation of the signalling of the line in 1986. 23 January 1993.

SOUTH WEST WALES

Above: **250. Brush Type 4** 47097 passes Llanelli goods shed as it approaches the station with a westbound tank train to Milford Haven. English Electric Type 3 37223 is on the left. 4 August 1987.

Opposite above: **251. In InterCity** livery, Brush Type 4 47501 departs from Llanelli with the 14.20 Milford Haven to Swansea. The station was opened as Llanelly in 1852 on the South Wales Railway's extension to Carmarthen. 4 August 1987.

Opposite below: **252. A few** miles west of Llanelli, the line to Cynheidre Colliery heads north from the main line to South West Wales. Here, F & W Railtours' 'The Valley Trekker' from Plymouth departs from the colliery behind 25325 and 33012, with 37234 on the rear of the train. The colliery, opened in 1954 in the Gwendraeth valley, was closed in 1989. 30 November 1985.

253. Brush Type 4 47501 approaches Pembrey and Burry Port with the 12.08 Swansea to Milford Haven. The former Pembrey East signal box, a GWR Type 7 design dating from 1907, is next to the level crossing in the background. 4 August 1987.

254. Class 101 DMU set S802, forming the 11.30 Milford Haven to Swansea, departs from Pembrey and Burry Port. The station was opened in 1852. 4 August 1987.

255. From Pembrey and Burry Port, a freight line ran to Coedbach Washery and on to Cwmmawr Colliery. Here, 08993 *Ashburnham* is pictured at Cwmmawr with the 8F00 15.00 to Coedbach. Because of the tight clearances on the Burry Port & Gwendraeth Valley Line, this locomotive, now preserved, was one of five Class 08 shunters with cut-down cabs that were used between Cwmmawr and Coedbach. 24 March 1992. (*Steve Turner Photo*)

256. Class 08 diesel-electric 08993 *Ashburnham* passes Pontyberem with the 8F00 15.00 Cwmmawr to Coedbach Washery. Pontyberem station opened in 1909 on the Burry Port and Gwendraeth Valley Railway. It was closed in 1953. 24 March 1992. (*Steve Turner Photo*)

257. Diesel-electric shunter 08993 *Ashburnham* crosses the B4309 and is about to pass the site of Pontyates railway station, closed in 1953, as it heads for Coedbach Washery with the 8F00 15.00 from Cwmmawr. 24 March 1992. (*Steve Turner Photo*)

258. British Railways Type 5 56032 *Sir De Morgannwg/County of South Glamorgan* heads away from Coedbach Washery with the 6E07 15.35 to Immingham. 18 May 1995. (*Steve Turner Photo*)

259. Class 119 Cross-Country DMU set C590, forming a westbound service, runs alongside the River Towy estuary at Ferryside, between Kidwelly and Carmarthen. 5 September 1987.

260. With two Royal Mail coaches behind the locomotive, Brush Type 4 47594 rounds the curve from Carmarthen Junction as it approaches Carmarthen with the 17.10 Swansea to Milford Haven. Carmarthen Junction signal box is in the background. 3 August 1987.

261. With Carmarthen station in the background, Brush Type 4 47609 *Fire Fly* shunts the 7B54 06.05 Severn Tunnel Junction to Fishguard Harbour pick-up freight in the yard. 4 August 1987.

262. Having replaced 47594 and with the Royal Mail coaches left in the platform, 37427 *Bont Y Bermo* passes the Brush Type 4 as it heads away from Carmarthen with the 17.10 Swansea to Milford Haven. In the yard, 37904 shunts the 7B57 pick-up goods from Fishguard Harbour. The train will later depart as the 7B03 to Severn Tunnel Junction. 3 August 1987.

263. With power car 43145 leading, InterCity 125 unit set 253 038, forming the 07.40 Milford Haven to London Paddington, rounds the curve from Carmarthen Bridge Junction and approaches Carmarthen station. 4 August 1987.

264. Passengers are waiting on the platform as Class 101 DMU set S802, forming a Pembroke Dock to Swansea service, arrives at Whitland. The station, opened in 1854, is located at the junction of the lines to Fishguard Harbour, Swansea, and Pembroke Dock. 2 August 1987.

265. Class 101 DMU set S807, forming a Swansea to Pembroke Dock service, arrives at Narberth, between Whitland and Tenby. 2 August 1987.

266. Class 101 DMU set C808, forming the 08.40 Cardiff Central to Pembroke Dock, crosses the seven-arch viaduct to the north of the station as it arrives at Tenby. 2 August 1987.

267. Class 101 DMU set C808, forming the 12.15 Pembroke Dock to Llanelli service, stands at Tenby station. The station was opened in 1866, while the station buildings and the cast iron canopy date from 1871. 2 August 1987.

268. Class 101 DMU set C808, forming the 12.15 Pembroke Dock to Llanelli service, arrives at Tenby station. The Western Region signal box was built in 1956, replacing an earlier box. It was closed in 1988. 2 August 1987.

269. The level crossing gates are opened while Class 101 DMU set S801 waits to enter Manorbier station. The working is the 15.45 Carmarthen to Pembroke Dock. The former station building is now a private residence. 2 August 1987.

270. A Metro-Cammell Class 101 DMU departs from Pembroke Dock station with a service to Swansea. The station was opened in 1864 by the Pembroke and Tenby Railway to serve the Royal Navy dockyard in the town. Until 1969, a freight line ran past the station to the dockside. 1 August 1987.

271. Taking the line to Fishguard Harbour and Milford Haven, Brush Type 4 47508 *SS Great Britain* heads west from Whitland with the 2B22 12.08 Swansea to Milford Haven. 3 August 1987.

272. The line to Fishguard Harbour diverges from the Swansea to Milford Haven line at Clarbeston Road. Here, InterCity 125 unit set 253 007, forming the 15.00 Fishguard Harbour to London Paddington, passes the station as it heads east towards Whitland. Clarbeston Road signal box, opposite the junction in the background, is a GWR Type 7c design, built in 1906. An entrance-exit (NX) panel was installed in the box in 1988. 2 August 1987.

273. British Rail Type 5 56048 heads a tank train from the Gulf Oil Refinery at Waterston, near Milford Haven, to Theale through Haverfordwest station. The station is located on the line to Milford Haven, between Clarbeston Road and Johnston. 3 August 1987.

274. Metro-Cammell Class 101 DMU set C823, forming a Milford Haven to Swansea service, passes the old goods shed as it departs from Haverfordwest. 1 August 1987.

275. Class 101 DMU set C823, forming a Swansea to Milford Haven service, arrives at Haverfordwest. Haverfordwest Station signal box was a GWR Type 12a design, opened in 1938. It was closed in 1988 when the line from Clarbeston Road was singled and the signalling was controlled from Clarbeston Road box. 1 August 1987.

276. Class 119 DMU set C583, forming a Swansea to Milford Haven service, arrives at Johnston. The station was opened in 1856 on the line from Haverfordwest to Neyland. It was the junction of the line to Neyland, closed in 1964, and the line to Milford Haven. 3 August 1987.

277. British Rail Type 5 56048 passes Johnston with an oil tank train to Robeston. The GWR Type 3 signal box dates from around 1885. It closed in 1988. 1 August 1987.

278. Class 101 DMU set S800, forming a Swansea service, waits for departure time at Milford Haven. The station, opened in 1863, was originally named Milford, becoming Milford Haven by 1910. Milford Haven is the terminus of one of the lines from Swansea. 1 August 1987.

279. Class 03 0-6-0 diesel-mechanical shunter 03113 is displayed at Milford Haven Harbour with a four-wheel tank wagon. The locomotive, now preserved at Rowsley, was sold to Gulf Oil, Milford Haven, after it was withdrawn by British Rail in 1975. Oil refineries were located at Robeston (Amoco) and Waterston (Gulf), near Milford Haven. 28 October 1995. (*Paul Dorney Photo*)

280. Fishguard and Goodwick station, opened in 1899, was the railway terminus at Fishguard until the GWR extended the line to Fishguard Harbour in 1906. The station was closed to passengers in 1964. Here, the InterCity 125 unit, forming the 12.40 Swansea to Fishguard Harbour service, passes the station. It was reopened in 2012. 2 August 1987.

281. With power car 43015 trailing, InterCity 125 unit set 253 007, forming the 12.40 Swansea to Fishguard Harbour service, approaches Fishguard Harbour station. From Fishguard, ferries cross the Irish Sea to Rosslare Harbour in Ireland. 2 August 1987.

STEAM-HAULED SPECIAL TRAINS

282. With the Castle carrying 'The Red Dragon' headboard, GWR Castle Class 4-6-0 5051 *Drysllwyn Castle* and GWR Modified Hall 4-6-0 6998 *Burton Agnes Hall*, both in Great Western livery, pass Little Mill Junction as they head for Newport with a special train from Hereford to Didcot. The Collett Castle was built at Swindon Works in May 1936 and withdrawn from service in May 1963 when it was sold to Woodham Brothers. It was the fourth locomotive to be removed from the scrapyard for preservation. The Hawksworth Modified Hall was also built at Swindon, in January 1949, and withdrawn in December 1965. It was purchased by the Great Western Society in January 1966. 28 June 1986.

Above: 283. Carrying 'The Red Dragon' headboard, Castle Class 4-6-0 5051 *Drysllwyn Castle* heads away from Abergavenny with a special train from Hereford to Swindon. Built in 1936, the locomotive was named *Drysllwyn Castle*. In August 1937, it was renamed *Earl Bathurst,* the name it would carry until it was withdrawn. The name *Drysllwyn Castle* was later applied to Castle Class locomotive 7018. 12 October 1985.

Opposite above: 284. GWR King Class 4-6-0 6000 *King George V* heads north at Cwmbran with a 'Welsh Marches Express' from Newport. Designed by Charles Collett, the locomotive was built in 1927 at Swindon Works. *King George V* visited North America in August 1927 for the Baltimore & Ohio Centenary, where it was presented with a brass bell and cabside medallions to mark the occasion. The locomotive is carrying a 'Cornish Riviera Express' headboard, the name of a Paddington to Penzance express which first ran in 1904. Withdrawn in 1962, the locomotive is owned by the National Railway Museum and is now displayed at Swindon. 24 March 1984.

Opposite below: 285. King Class 4-6-0 6024 *King Edward I* passes East Usk Yard at Newport with the return leg of the Evening Post and Western Daily Press 'Severnsider' Bristol to Newport excursion. The locomotive, built at Swindon in 1930, was withdrawn in 1962 and sold to Woodham Brothers' scrapyard at Barry. Thirty members of the class were built between 1927 and 1930. A replacement for 6007 *King William III* was built in 1936 following an accident near Shrivenham. *King Edward I* was bought for preservation in 1974 and returned to steam in 1989. 4 April 1994.

286. In 1985, various events were organised to commemorate the 150th anniversary of the founding of the Great Western Railway in 1835. One of the events saw GWR 2-8-0 2857 haul a freight train from Alexandra Dock Junction Yard into Newport station. Here the train is heading away from the yard towards the Hillfield Tunnels. The freight locomotive, designed by George Jackson Churchward, was built in 1918. After withdrawal in April 1963, it went to Woodham Brothers' scrapyard at Barry. It was purchased in May 1974 by the 2857 Society and arrived at the Severn Valley Railway in August 1975 for restoration. 10 September 1985.

287. In 1991, a number of special trains ran in connection with the 150th anniversary of the Taff Vale Railway. Here, British Railways Standard Class 4 2-6-4T 80080 departs from Barry Docks station with the return leg of a special train from Cardiff Central to Barry Docks. Designed by R.A. Riddles, the locomotive was built at Brighton Works in 1954. It was withdrawn from service in June 1965 and rescued from Barry Scrapyard in November 1980. The Vale of Glamorgan Council building, the former headquarters of the Barry Dock and Railway Company, is on the left. 6 October 1991.

288. Standard Class 4 2-6-4T 80080 heads west from Ystrad Rhondda with a special train from Cardiff Central to Treherbert. The train ran in connection with the 150th anniversary of the Taff Vale Railway. The headboard reads 'Taff Vale Railway 150'. 6 October 1991.

289. British Railways Standard Class 4 2-6-4T 80079 departs from Llandrindod Wells, on the Central Wales Line, with a special train from Shrewsbury to Carmarthen. The locomotive, built in 1954 at Brighton Works, was withdrawn in July 1965, after which it was taken to Barry Scrapyard, reaching there in the January of the following year. It arrived at the Severn Valley Railway in May 1971, where it is still based. 16 May 1993.

POSTSCRIPT

Finally, we briefly look, in more recent times, at various operational preservation locations relating to closed railways of South Wales. In addition to the locations illustrated here, the Garw Valley Railway is working to restore the former GWR line between Pontycymer and Brynmenyn and has the intention of creating a heritage centre at Pontycymer in conjunction with the Garw Heritage Society.

290. The Big Pit National Coal Museum. The Big Pit at Blaenavon, closed in 1980, was served by coal trains running from Llantarnam Junction on the line from Newport to Pontypool. The mine was opened to the public in 1983. Two industrial saddle tanks can be seen in this general view of the site. On the left is 0-6-0ST PD No. 10 (Hudswell Clarke 544 of 1900). The locomotive spent its working life in Wales, finishing at Coedely Coking Plant. The other locomotive is The Blaenavon Co Ltd 0-4-0ST *Nora* No. 5 (Andrew Barclay 1680 of 1920). 14 September 2014.

291. The Pontypool and Blaenavon Railway. The Pontypool and Blaenavon Railway is a heritage railway running for 3½ miles from Blaenavon to a halt at the Whistle Inn public house. Big Pit halt, on the site of a former colliery furnace, serves The Big Pit National Coal Museum. The line runs on the trackbed of the Brynmawr and Blaenavon Railway, opened in 1866. Here, 0-4-0ST *Sir Thomas Royden* (Andrew Barclay 2088 of 1940) climbs the bank from Blaenavon High Level towards Furnace Sidings with a short demonstration freight train. The locomotive previously worked at Stourport Power Station and was visiting from Rocks by Rail, the Living Ironstone Museum at Cottesmore. 14 September 2014.

292. The Brecon Mountain Railway. The Brecon Mountain Railway is a 1ft 11¾in narrow gauge railway on the south side of the Brecon Beacons. It runs from Pant, two miles north of Merthyr Tydfil, along the trackbed of the former Brecon and Merthyr Railway to Torpantau station. Here, 0-6-2WTT *Graf Schwerin-Löwitz* (Arnold Jung 1261 of 1908) approaches Pontsticill station with a train from Pant. 16 September 2008.

Above: **293. The Teifi** Valley Railway. The 2ft gauge Teifi Valley Railway ran for just under 2 miles, between Henllan and a demolished bridge over the Afon Teifi, along the trackbed of the former GWR line between Llandysul and Newcastle Emlyn. In 2014 the railway was closed but since 2016 it is being progressively reopened. Here, Kerr, Stuart 0-6-2T *Sgt Murphy* (3117 of 1918) runs round its train at Henllan station. Built for wartime use, it was used by the Admiralty at Beachley Dock at Chepstow after the First World War. It later worked at Penrhyn Quarry. 13 August 2009.

Opposite above: **294. The Llanelli** & Mynydd Mawr Railway. Cynheidre Colliery was closed in 1989, but in September 2017, the Llanelli and Mynydd Mawr Railway was opened to the public on the site of the old colliery. The name was taken from the original name of the railway with the spelling of Llanelly changed to Llanelli. During a public open day in June 2021, rides along a section of reinstated track were given using a Pacer DMU. Here, Class 142 Pacer 142 006 approaches the small station at Cynheidre as it returns from a trip along the line, past the site of the old colliery. Class 143 Pacer 143 607 is on the left with 143 606 on the right. The line is to be extended at a later date. 26 June 2021.

Opposite below: **295. The Barry** Tourist Railway. The railway runs from Barry Island to a small station at the old goods shed at Hood Road, Barry. On the occasion of my visit in 2021, because of Covid 19 restrictions, the railway was offering brake van rides for a short distance up the bank from the goods shed towards Barry station. The former goods shed, on the right, has been converted into hospitality and retail units. Here the train is approaching the station before the first service of the day. The locomotive is Kerr, Stuart & Co Ltd 0-4-0WT 3063 of 1918, which previously worked at the National Shipyard at Chepstow. 17 July 2021.

296. The Gwili Railway. The railway runs for four miles from the site of Abergwili Junction, near Carmarthen, along the route of the former Carmarthen to Aberystwyth line, to Danycoed. The original railway was closed in 1965 but in 1978, the Gwili Railway Preservation Company started operating trains from its base at Bronwydd Arms. It was the first standard gauge preserved railway to operate in Wales. Here, visiting GWR 5700 Class 0-6-0 pannier tank L92, in London Transport livery, approaches Bronwydd Arms station with a train from Abergwili Junction. The locomotive was built at Swindon Works in 1930 to the design of Charles Collett and was sold to London Transport in 1958, where it worked as L92 until 1969. After withdrawal it was sold to the Worcester Locomotive Society. 26 June 2021.

297. The Gwili Railway. The level crossing gates on the B4301 road are closed to trains at Bronwydd Arms station, headquarters of the Gwili Railway. When the railway was closed in 1965, the station building and signal box were demolished. The replacement station building was built using Llandovery signal box from the Central Wales line and the signal box was recovered from Llandybie on the same line. 26 June 2021.

BIBLIOGRAPHY

Baker, S.K., *Rail Atlas Great Britain and Ireland*, Haynes Publishing Group, 1980 and 1988

British Rail, *British Rail Passenger Timetable(s)*, May 1984-October 1993, British Railways Board, 1984-1993

Gradients of the British Main Line Railways, Ian Allan Publishing Ltd, 2016

Jowett, A., *Jowett's Railway Atlas of Great Britain and Ireland*, Patrick Stephens Ltd, 1989

Marsden, C., *35 Years of Main Line Diesel Traction*, Oxford Publishing Co., 1982

Page, J., *Forgotten Railways South Wales*, David and Charles, 1979

Signalling Study Group, *The Signal Box, A Pictorial History*, Oxford Publishing Co., 1986

Wood, R., *British Rail Locomotives*, Ian Allan Ltd, 1986

INDEX TO LOCATIONS BY PHOTO NUMBERS